Table of Contents

Introduction   5

Things to Consider Before Purchasing a Puppy   7

Equipment   9

Feeding Your Puppy   10

When Is the Best Time to Train Your Puppy?   12

The Stages of Puppy Development   13

Basic Training   15

Teaching the Puppy Its Name   16

Teaching the Puppy to Sit   17

Teaching the Puppy to Lie Down   18

Teaching the Puppy to Stay and Come When Called   19

Teaching Your Puppy to Heel   20

How to Train Your Puppy Not to Jump Up   22

How to Train Your Puppy to Not Jump/Paw Your Guests   25

How to Train Your Puppy Not to Cry or Whine When You're Gone   26

Dealing with Separation Anxiety   28

Stopping Excessive Barking   30

How to Crate Train Your Puppy   33

How to Potty Train Your Puppy without a Crate   37

How to Train Your Puppy Not to Pee in the House   39

How to Train Your Puppy Not to Bite   41

How to Train Your Puppy to Walk on a Leash   43

Puppy Games and Tricks   45

A Final 'Paws' for Thought   47

Introduction

A dog is often described as "man's best friend" and any decision to purchase a dog or puppy should be given careful consideration. Many potential owners are often drawn into owning a dog after seeing a cute puppy and subsequently give very little thought to how the dog will develop and the commitments that will need to be made in the future.

Owning a dog will require a significant amount of time and money over a number of years. Some dogs will live into their teens so anyone considering a dog as a pet should factor this into their decision. For those people not wanting to commit to the longevity and commitment of nurturing and training a puppy may want to consider buying an older dog from a rescue centre or animal shelter.

This option has its benefits in that the animal will more than likely have had some kind of training and depending on its age it could be fully trained. But it is important to remember that the dog is in the shelter for a reason, so don't be afraid to do a little research and ask about its history. Check the previous owner and their reasons for not wanting the dog anymore. It may be that the dog belonged to an older person that passed away and is simply looking for a new home. If this is the case, then it may be a more suitable alternative to buying a puppy.

Before taking ownership of any kind of dog, it's important to consider the following things as dog ownership has many responsibilities:

You must be willing to commit the next 10 to 15 years of your life to care and provide for the animal.

The owner must be prepared to dedicate a considerable amount of time towards the dogs training needs and exercise routines.

Consider your ambitions and plans for the future. Do you have any intentions of working abroad or starting a family? These issues will impact on the dog and should be considered if the owner has plans to change their lifestyle in the foreseeable future.

Are you the right type of person to have a dog? Do not consider having a dog if you have commitment issues or get bored easily.

Can you cope with the physical and financial demands that come with owning a dog? The dog will need to be exercised daily and food, vet bills and grooming all cost money.

For those people still wanting to purchase a puppy it's important to prepare and research certain things before making any commitment to buying.

Things to Consider Before Purchasing a Puppy

Picking the Right Breed

You will need to decide on whether you go for a mixed breed dog or pure breed (pedigree) dog. Certain breeds have a good reputation for being family dogs whereas other breeds can have aggressive characteristics and be more territorial. It's important to research the breed thoroughly and don't be afraid to discuss any issues with your local vet as they will be able to provide information on any particular breed of dog that you are considering. When you have made your decision then start looking for a reputable breeder and be prepared to wait for the right one to come along.

Male or Female

Choosing the sex of your dog may be influenced by any decision to breed from it in the future but in general, female dogs (normally referred to as bitches) are considered to be less territorial and easier to train than male dogs. Many owners decide to get their dog or puppy spayed or castrated at a young age if they have no future breeding aspirations in order to avoid any potential accidents or acts of sexually aggression.

Size

Dogs come in all shapes and sizes and seeing the animal in its puppy form is not always a good indicator for future growth, so researching this area is important. If your property has lots of living space and a big garden, then you might decide that a bigger dog is for you, but if space is limited, it might be worth considering a smaller dog that takes up less space.

Sleeping Arrangements

Dogs are territorial by nature and it's often a good idea to identify a space and allocate it as the dogs sleeping area. Most dogs tend to like confined spaces so look at setting up a space under the stairs or in a corner so that when the dog wants some quiet time it can retreat to its bed.

Find a Vet

Find a local vet and discuss your situation with them. They will be able to confirm what inoculations the puppy will need and how much it will all cost. They may also help with recommending a particular breed of dog that suits your lifestyle or they may even recommend a breeder that has puppies for sale.

Dog Obedience Classes

Some puppies can be trained without the need for classes but a lot will depend on the owner and the puppy's willingness to learn. If you decide to try obedience classes, then discuss the situation with your local vet and do some research do find out what is available in your area.

Equipment

Once you have decided that a puppy is for you then it's important to purchase the right equipment before you bring the puppy home. Consider buying the following:

Food and water bowls – try stainless steel as they do not chip or break as easily as other alternatives

Food – check with the puppy supplier as to the type of food they used in the initial few weeks as it's always best to remain consistent and avoid drastic changes to their diet.

A pet gate or child's stair gate – having this item will allow you to enclose certain areas in the house and will stop the puppy from running wild. This will prove particularly useful when toilet training the puppy.

Toys – puppies love toys and it's important to have a varied selection to offer. Chewy toys are important for the puppy in its teething and chewing stage whereas balls and squeaky toys are great for playing games with.

A bed for the puppy to sleep on.

FEEDING YOUR PUPPY

Puppies grow quicker than adult dogs and as such they require a particular type of diet to assist with their expansion.

Most puppies will need feeding at least 4 times a day up until they reach the age of 4 months, that amount should be reduced to 3 times a day up until 6 months and then after that the puppy should be fed twice a day for the rest of its life.

There is a variety of food available for dogs and puppies and a good dog breeder should advise what's best for the puppy in the first few months, but if you are unsure you should consult your vet. When choosing the correct type of food for your dog or puppy you should select a product that is easily digested and avoid changing this unnecessarily.

Listed below are the four main types of food available:

Dry Complete Foods

Certain puppies will struggle to adapt to dry food immediately after weaning, but they will develop a liking for this type of food over time. If the puppy does struggle to adapt, then try adding a little water or tinned food to the dried mix to soften it up.

There is a wide range of dry complete foods on the market and its best to avoid the cheaper brands if you can as they will contain low quality ingredients which will result in problems. Spending a little extra on a better quality product will benefit the dog as the food will be more nutritional and you will probably find that the dog will use less of it.

Semi-Moist and Tinned Foods

Like the dried food, the semi-moist and tinned varieties can vary in quality and it's important to select something with a high nutritional value.

Home-Made Food

Try to avoid giving the puppy too much home cooked food in its early life as this can upset the puppy and may cause problems. Whilst a home cooked meal may appear healthy to a human, it won't necessarily be healthy for a puppy.

Avoid sudden changes to the dog's diet as stability is important.

Treats

Treats are a good tool to use when rewarding and training and not all treats have to be the unhealthy kind. Visit your local pet store and research the ingredients of the various treats on offer and try to steer clear of products that have a high sugar and fat content as there are a number of healthy doggy treats on the market.

When Is the Best Time to Train Your Puppy?

Theoretically, a puppy will start learning new things from the moment they are born, but most owners will not get the chance to apply training methods until they bring their dog home at the 7 – 8 week stage. This is considered to be the best time to start training your new pet and it is essential to get the dog into good habits early on in its life to stand the best chance of producing a well-behaved animal.

Most experts believe that the first 4 months of a puppy's life is a critical stage in the training process as they are generally better at learning new skills and experiences due to their brain development.

The Stages of Puppy Development

The first 2 months of a puppy's life will be spent with its mother and any other puppies that were delivered at the time. During this time it will experience its first lessons in social contact, playtime and discipline through interaction with the mother and other siblings.

After the initial 7-8 week stage with its mother the puppy will be introduced to its new home and family. This is an extremely significant period of time as the foundations for future temperament and character will be formed by the end of the 4 month period and mistakes at this stage can cause problems in the future. During this crucial time it is important to tackle the issues of toilet training, discourage biting and chewing as well as establishing ground rules for the puppy in respect of the use of furniture and sleeping arrangements.

During this stage of the puppy's life it will probably encounter some kind of fear or phobia of a particular object or event. These fears can have a lasting consequence if not dealt with correctly as the dog will develop a long-term apprehension towards whatever has caused the problem. Deal with the issue in a positive and firm manner without offering any form of praise or sympathy towards the animal.

After the first 4 months the puppy will find its feet and settle into its new environment. It will probably want to establish its place in the pecking order of the family unit. At this stage it is important that the senior members of the family retain the power in the relationship and remain consistent in the training methods used in the first 4 months.

The subsequent 12 -14 months of the animals life will see a physical change where the puppy grows and develops into a full-sized dog, but during that period it will also endure other changes that will affect its behavior. At some point during the first 6 months of its life the puppy will lose its milk teeth and gain adult teeth. This will result in a chewing phase which may last a few months so be prepared to maintain the training methods used previously. It may prove useful to purchase teething rings and other chewy toys to offer the puppy an alternative to chewing the legs on the dining room table.

After the first year the dog will develop a maturity and become less boisterous and you should be able to see a benefit to all of the training and hard work from the previous year. You may notice that the dog develops the occasional fear in respect of new circumstances and may show an unwillingness to approach new people or new things. As before, the issue should be dealt with in a calm, down-to-earth way, without offering praise or sympathy.

Basic Training

Training a puppy involves two basic types of training: behavioral and obedience.

The first of these methods focuses on the prevention and improvement of bad behavior or conduct. It is important to remain consistent with all aspects of behavior training as inconsistencies will create confusion in the puppy.

Obedience training concentrates on getting the dog to follow specific commands like sit and stay. This type of training should be conducted regularly but only for 10 – 15 minute sessions at a time to help avoid boredom. To assist with obedience training you may also want to consider training before meals as the food on offer will increase their concentration levels.

Let's now take a look at the basic commands we can use.

Teaching the Puppy Its Name

Before any formal training begins it's important that your dog knows its name. Most owners will decide on a name before they take ownership of the puppy, but if you have not, then it is best not to leave it too long before deciding. Using the name is vital and it is important to use the name with every command with the exception of "no" and "stay".

Teaching the Puppy to Sit

A common technique that will help teach your puppy to sit will involve the use of rewards. The practice involves taking a treat and placing your hand (with the treat in it) above the puppy's head. The dog will naturally look up towards the treat and it is then that the owner should issue the command "sit" whilst gently encouraging the dog to sit with their other hand. Within a short time the dog will associate sitting with receiving a reward and will complete the process without any kind of assistance or use of treat.

When practicing this method it is important to remember that lessons should be brief and often.

Teaching the Puppy to Lie Down

Teaching the dog to lie uses a similar method to the sitting technique. Again, a reward is used to focus the dog. Tell the dog to sit and hold the reward in the air. Then bring the hand down to floor level and instruct the dog with "down" with a strong command.

Allow the dog to have the reward if the process has been completed correctly and repeat this exercise regularly in conjunction with the sitting technique.

Teaching the Puppy to Stay and Come When Called

Once you have mastered the sit and lie commands it's time to move onto training the dog to stay and come when called. Its best to conquer the sitting technique before attempting this area as you will find that the dog will stay better when sat.

The first stage of the process will involve getting the dog to sit. Do this in the normal way but this time make a point of having two rewards in your hand. Offer the first reward when the dog sits and hold your hand up whilst slowly and clearly instructing the dog to "stay". Then start retreating away from the dog making sure you face them at all times. When you have managed to retreat a short distance issue the command "come" and lower your hand. If the dog completes the task successfully, then issue the treat and praise the dog, but if they move before the "come" instruction is issued, then avoid rewarding the dog and start the process again.

When the dog begins to grasp the concept of "stay" and "come" you should look to increase the distance between you and the dog before issuing the "come" command.

Teaching Your Puppy to Heel

Teaching a puppy to heel is a slightly more advanced technique than the others listed above. This type of training involves the puppy walking very close to the owner (either on or off the leash) and should be used in situations where other dogs, children and traffic are in close proximity.

Heel training involves lots of concentration and repetition and should only be practiced for short periods at a time as it is important to have the dog's complete attention.

To begin with, stand with the puppy on your left leg with both you and the dog looking the same way.

Hold a treat in you left hand, making sure that you do not hold it too close to the dog. Call the dog by name to get its attention and take two steps forward. If the dog follows and remains in position, then actively praise it and offer the treat.

After successfully completing the process you should continue to repeat, but make sure that the praise and reward method is only used when the dog remains in the heel position.

At this stage it is important to understand that the reward should only being used to reward his behavior and not tempt or encourage the dog in anyway. Do not offer the reward or praise if the dog begins to stray.

When the dog becomes comfortable with heeling over 2 steps, it will be time to increase the number of steps to 4. Follow the same procedure but offer the praise and reward after the fourth step.

Continue to repeat this process and move to 6 steps, then 8 and so on when the dog starts to master the process.

When the dog reaches a consistent level of heeling and you are able to practice over a distance of 10 steps then it's time to assign a verbal command to the process. Use the same process as before but this time call the name of the dog followed by the "heel" and move forward.

The dog should now have grasped the basics of heeling and in time and with continuous training his ability to heel should improve. Consider adding a couple of changes to the training process if the dog shows enthusiasm: try increasing or decreasing the speed at which you walk, try new locations and increase the length of time you keep the dog heeled.

How to Train Your Puppy Not to Jump Up

It's a natural instinct for most puppies to want to jump up and whilst it will appear fun and harmless during the early months it will become a problem when the dog grows and gets stronger.

There are two main reasons why a dog or puppy will jump up. The first is to offer some form of greeting to its owner or even another dog and the second will be to attract attention by trying to reach its owner's face.

One of the main things to consider when training the puppy to not jump is that the dog will be looking for affection when it greets you and it's therefore very important that the owner offers no form of attention until the dog is grounded. The two key points to remember when using this method are:

– Do not interact with the dog in anyway if they jump – do not instruct him/her to "get off" or push them away. Simply ignore him/her and if the jumping persists then walk away.

– Immediately offer acknowledgement and praise when the dog is grounded – even if they have persisted with the jumping for a length of time it is important that the owner acknowledges the dog when it does the right thing to help the animal understand the difference between right and wrong.

When using this method it is important to recognize that it is your attention and contact with the puppy that drives their understanding of what is considered acceptable.

In addition to the above there are also a couple of other techniques that can be used to assist with the jumping problem. Let's take a closer a look at these techniques.

Using a similar method to the one listed above, when the dog starts to jump, remain still and avoid using your arms or hands to push the dog off. Simply instruct the dog with "off" and turn away from him or her so they cannot reach your face. Instruct the dog to "sit" and when the dog follows your command kneel down and offer some mild and composed praise. Repeat the process whenever the dog jumps and it will eventually associate sitting down with receiving praise and affection.

Another method that uses the "sit" command can be adopted when entering a room. If the dog jumps up when you walk into the room, merely step back outside and shut the door. When outside of the room open the door slightly and instruct the dog to sit. If the dog sits then return to the room and offer gentle praise by kneeling down and stroking the dog. As before, repeat the process whenever the dog jumps.

A slightly different technique that can be used to overcome jumping involves the same process of entering the room. When the dog jumps, simply stand still and avoid eye contact. Say "off" and take a couple of quick steps towards the animal whilst making sure you avoid treading on the dog's paws. When the dog retreats out of the way and the front paws touch the ground tell it to "sit" and when it follows the command kneel down and stroke the dog. Again, it is important to repeat the technique when the dog offends.

Feel free to adapt any of the methods listed above to suite you or your dog as it may be that your dog responds better to playing with a certain toy than receiving praise through contact. If this is the case, then don't be afraid to use the toy as part of the reward process as the main objective is allow the dog to associate not jumping with praise and affection.

Let's now take a look at the things to avoid when greeting your puppy.

Try to avoid getting too excited when greeting your dog as it will only excite the animal and prolong the exercise. Staying relaxed and calm will promote calmness within the dog which will assist when training.

Try not to shout and raise your voice towards the dog as this will only cause excitement.

Avoid grabbing or pushing the dog away when training as this will have a negative effect. It's likely that the dog will treat the exercise as a game if it receives this kind of reaction and it will cause more jumping.

Do not try to inflict any pain or hurt towards the dog if it jumps. Cruelty towards any animal is unacceptable and it will not assist with the training in anyway.

HOW TO TRAIN YOUR PUPPY TO NOT JUMP/PAW YOUR GUESTS

When you feel that the dog has grasped the idea of not jumping, it may be worthwhile enlisting the help of friends or family to help you train the dog to welcome guests respectfully.

Before commencing any kind of training you will need to explain your preferred method of guidance to your family/friends and allow them to practice by entering the house in the normal way. After the guest has rung the bell or knocked on the door the dog will probably become excited and start barking. The owner will gain control of the situation by taking the dog towards the dog and telling it to "sit".

Open the door and allow the guest to enter the house. If the dog jumps up, then your guest will need to turn their back in the normal way and leave the room or house, closing the door behind them. If the dog remains seated the guest can acknowledge the dog and the owner can lavish praise and offer treats for successfully completing the process. Continue to practice this method with various people and don't be afraid to repeat it even when the dog appears to be getting it right.

How to Train Your Puppy Not to Cry or Whine When You're Gone

Many puppies will struggle to adapt when being left alone for long periods of time as they are simply not used to it. This type of behavior is commonly known as separation anxiety and is common in dogs of all ages.

Dogs and puppies that suffer from separation anxiety will express symptoms such as whining, crying, barking, chewing, digging and in some more severe cases they will take to destroying and damaging the home. In situations like this it is important to identify the cause of the problem as being separation anxiety and not just misbehavior as the 2 issues should be dealt with in a completely different way.

To gain a better understanding of the problem it's worth looking at it from the dog's perspective. From birth the dog has always been part of a family or pack environment. At first that would have been with its mother and other members of the litter and then after a short time the puppy would have been introduced into its new family environment with its new owner. During this transitional period the family will spend a large amount of time training and caring for the puppy, but at some point the dog will be required to be left on its own.

At this time the dog may become confused, stressed and nervous and show symptoms of separation anxiety because all it wants to do is socialize and spend time with its owner.

To help avoid separation anxiety a dog has to feel happy, safe and content within its surroundings whilst the owner is away. A key factor in conquering the anxiety is giving them things to do whilst you are out. Things like toys and treats will help ease their fears and lessen the boredom.

Dealing with Separation Anxiety

It is impossible to train your dog to not cry or whine when you leave, but it is important to tackle the issue and overcome its fear of abandonment. The dog needs to understand that there is no reason to get upset as you will return.

One way of helping the dog overcome its fear is to make a point of exiting and returning regularly throughout the day as this will help them get used to you departing and help them understand that you will return. When using this method it's always a good idea to increase the times of separation throughout the day.

This technique will help the dog understand that its fear is unjustified and you will be back. When returning it is important that you don't make a fuss of the dog and make a big thing about coming in and out as the dog needs to understand that you leaving the house is a normal occurrence and should not be feared.

An additional hint to help overcome problems with separation involves giving the dog plenty of exercise before leaving. This is something to consider if you intend on regularly leaving your dog for a length of time due to work commitments for example. Take the dog on a long walk or give it lots of playtime before you leave as the dog is more inclined to sleep whilst you are out, but be sure to give the dog the chance to calm down before you leave and do not make a fuss when you go.

Let's take a look at some of the things to avoid when you leave.

Do not lock the dog in a room when you go out as this will only create more tension and nervousness – give them as much space as possible.

Avoid lengthy farewells with the dog as this will only highlight their loneliness when you leave and may excite them to the point that they want to play. This will have a negative effect on the situation as the dog will look to exert its energy whilst you are out and could lead to the dog chewing or constantly barking.

Do not return if the dog starts to whine or cry when you leave as this will create a situation in itself.

Do not leave bones or chews as a form of treat or toy to keep the dog occupied when you are out as these can be dangerous.

Finally, avoid punishing the dog in an attempt to treat separation anxiety.

Stopping Excessive Barking

Barking is a completely natural thing for a dog to do and dealing with it can be a tricky and prolonged task. It's important that the dog owner realizes that it will be impossible to stop the dog from barking altogether and there will be times when a dog's bark will be welcomed.

It is important to establish the reason for the dog barking and identify the excessive barking that will eventually cause problems. There are numerous reasons why a dog will bark excessively and these are:

– Trying to communicate

– Part of the dog's breed or personality

– Marking territory

– To warn others of danger or a threat

– As a result of excitement and play (mainly with puppies)

– Barking at other creatures/animals

– If they feel cut off, isolated or trapped

– After separation from family or pack

– As a show of power or dominance

– As a result of previously being rewarded by their owners

– Lack of physical and intellectual stimulation

– Lack of proper socialization

– Looking for attention

It is important that the puppy understands that it is ok to bark at the right times but must be quiet when told. A useful technique to stop the dog from barking is to instruct them "be quiet" whilst holding out a treat. The dog will inevitably stop barking in an attempt to sniff out the treat. When the dog goes quiet you should offer praise and reward the dog with the treat after a few seconds.

During the course of this training exercise it is important to remain consistent and only offer the treat when the dog remains quiet. As time passes it's important to increase the times between the "be quiet" commands and offering the treat.

One of the biggest mistakes us dog owners make is to inadvertently reward our dogs excessive barking. We actually encourage and reinforce the barking problem when we commit the following three dog training sins:

Avoid Shouting

Ty to avoid shouting at the dog when it barks as this will only give them the attention that they crave. This will also have the adverse effect on the training as it's likely that the dog will think that you are joining in.

Avoid Following the Dog's Request

If the dog is barking to be let back inside or let out then avoid doing what they ask as it will only reinforce their request and make them think that it is ok to bark. Wait till they stop barking then take action.

Avoid Rewarding the Dog

Do not respond to barking with a reward or any other form of positive reaction in an attempt to silence the dog as this will only encourage incorrect behavior.

How to Crate Train Your Puppy

Crate training is an exercise that teaches the puppy to recognize a crate (sometimes referred to as a cage) as part of its home. The puppy is encouraged to use the crate when sleeping and when the owners are not around. Those people that support crate training often continue to use this method after the puppy stage has elapsed as they believe that because dogs are considered to be den dwelling animals, they are happy to use the crate as a den replacement. Others on the other hand consider the idea of locking a dog in a cage to be cruel.

Whatever your opinion is on the matter there is no arguing about the effectiveness of using this method for potty training during the puppy stage, but before we look at the method in detail it is important to understand that leaving a puppy (or dog) in a crate for long periods of time can have a negative effect on the process and could result in the puppy becoming anxious, destructive and unhappy.

The crate training method focuses on the fact that dogs like confined spaces and feel more at ease and secure when they know they have a safe place to sleep. This method also plays on the fact that dogs will always look to avoid soiling or urinating on their own sleeping area so will be more inclined to hold onto their urge or let you know that they want to go. Obviously, in the early stages of crate training it is important to acknowledge that there will be accidents and that it is important to give the puppy the opportunity to go outside regularly to do their toilet business as they are unable to control their bladder.

Let's now take a look at the things to consider when using the crate training method.

Buying the Crate

When purchasing a crate you will need to decide if you are buying for the short or long term. For those owners that intend to continue using this method throughout the dog's life they may wish to consider buying a bigger crate that can house a full-sized dog. In this situation it will also be necessary to buy a divider for the crate as it is important to not give the dog too much room in the crate whilst potty training in the early stages.

If you intend on using the crate for the sole purpose of training a puppy, then you will only need to buy a crate big enough to house the puppy. The crate should be big enough to hold the puppy's bed and have enough room inside to allow the puppy to stand, stretch and turn around.

It is important that the owner avoids buying an oversized crate as this will give the puppy the opportunity to find a space that they can use for toilet duties.

Introducing the Crate

It is important to introduce the puppy to the crate as early as possible, but do it gradually as the process should not be rushed. Begin by introducing the crate into the room. Then try putting the dog's toys inside and encourage it to go in. Then place its food bowl and water bowl inside and encourage it to eat and drink within the crate. When the dog is happy, try persuading it to go inside and encourage it to spend time by laying the bed out in the crate. At this stage we will continue to leave the crate door open.

Eventually the dog will gain confidence in using the crate and will willingly use it independently. This is a key achievement in the process as it is important that the puppy is comfortable with its new environment.

Closing the Door and Bedtime

When the puppy is happy to enter the crate independently it will be time to try shutting the crate door. At first, the dog may express its displeasure by barking or whining, but it's important to not give in straight away by letting it out. Doing this will only indicate to the dog that when it gets upset in the crate, it will be let out after making a fuss. In this instance, only let the dog out when it has settled.

Continue with the process and keep increasing the length of time the puppy spends in the crate to increase familiarization. At this stage it is also important that the owner/trainer spends time away from the puppy whilst it is in the crate to allow it to get used to being on its own.

Once the dog has accepted its new surroundings and appears happy to spend more than 30 minutes in the crate with nobody around, then it will be the right time to try crate training through the night.

If everything has gone according to plan with the day-time crate training it should be relatively straight forward to overcome any issues with bedtime. The important thing to remember here is that putting the puppy to bed needs to be made into a routine where the puppy is given the opportunity to let off steam with some playtime. Then afterwards the puppy should be offered the chance to go outside to go to toilet before it is put into the crate for bedtime.

When the dog returns from its toilet visit it should be encouraged into the crate with a treat and left to settle with minimal attention. If the dog protests, then it's important to not let it out of the crate unless you think it requires the toilet. If this is the case, then let it out to do its business and offer no attention when it returns. Simply instruct the puppy back into the crate.

If the puppy persists with whining or crying, then be prepared to ignore them as surrendering at this stage will only cause a setback and allow the puppy to think that they have won the battle. If the puppy continues to show resistance, try putting a blanket over the crate to block out light or try moving the crate to another area of the house.

The majority of dogs will stop using their crate for one reason or another as they get older. Some will opt for sleeping in a particular part of the house instead of the crate, whereas others will be encouraged to stop by their owners. Occasionally a dog will become very attached to its crate and continue using it for years.

How to Potty Train Your Puppy without a Crate

Not all dog owners adopt the crate training method as some believe that the use of the crate restricts the dog's movement. Also, in some instances certain dogs struggle with the use of the crate because they develop a fear after suffering from a previous bad experience.

A puppy is similar to a baby in many respects in that it has very little control of its bladder in its infant years and cannot be expected to hold on. It is important that the owner accepts that there will be accidents as potty training a puppy requires a persistent and consistent approach.

A popular alternative to the crate method is paper training. This method is best used in conjunction with regular outdoor visits, but it basically involves laying newspaper on a hard floor (preferably tiled or laminated) and encouraging the puppy to use the papered area to perform toilet duties.

Once a suitable area in the house has been established it is important to enclose this space and put the dog's bed in this area and cover the remaining area with paper. The general idea is the same as crate training in that the dog will not want to soil or urinate its own bed so will be forced to use the paper.

When the puppy grasps the idea and starts using the paper regularly, it is important to offer plenty of praise and then gradually reduce the size of the papered area. The key aspect to this training method is to get the puppy to associate going to toilet with the paper.

When accidents occur it is important to not punish or shout at the puppy after the event has happened as the dog will have no idea what it has done wrong. If you catch the puppy going in the wrong area, then simply issue a command of "no" and place the dog on the paper to finish off.

In time and with regular outdoor visits, the puppy will development better bladder and bowel control and the paper will be used on a less frequent basis. Keep a look out for signs such as pacing, sniffing and waiting at the door to determine when to take the dog out and create routines of letting the dog out at regular intervals.

The disadvantage of paper training a puppy is that you are effectively allowing the puppy to go to toilet indoors and as such your dog may not fully accept that going outside is the right thing to do. Whilst this method is not as effective as the Crate Training method it can be successful and is often adopted by owners who have a limited amount of time. This method also requires less effort as opposed to Crate Training. Saying that, be prepared that it is still going to take some time to achieve the goal.

How to Train Your Puppy Not to Pee in the House

No matter what method you decide to use when potty training your puppy, the key elements are the same. The overall objective is to get the puppy to accept that the idea of going to toilet in the house is wrong and build a routine that allows the puppy to go outside and eliminate regularly.

Key points to remember:

Potty training will require a lot of time and effort – the puppy may grasp the idea of going to toilet outside within a couple of weeks, but it may take months to train them properly.

Be consistent with the training and never allow your frustration to show.

Build a routine that gives the puppy regular opportunities to relieve themselves outdoors. Try to construct the schedule around meal times (avoid feeding at bedtime) and naps ensuring the dog has the chance to eliminate first thing in the morning, before bedtime and after meal times.

Watch for signs that indicate that the dog may need to go out. Sniffing, pacing, whining and lurking by the door are often good indictors that the puppy needs the toilet.

Avoid giving the puppy too much freedom in the early stages. Try to restrict them to one or two rooms in the house at the beginning of the training and always leave paper on the floor if you decide against crate training the puppy.

Accept that there will be accidents and always offer praise when the puppy does well.

How to Train Your Puppy Not to Bite

Many puppies will go through a biting or chewing stage and this is perfectly normal as it helps to keep their teeth and gums healthy. Whilst the biting and chewing stage is associated with puppies, the majority of dogs will continue to enjoy a good chew as they get older. The key aspect of training the puppy not to bite is to persuade and praise the puppy for chewing and biting the right items.

The first thing to address when dealing with this problem will be to make sure that the puppy has plenty of chew toys. Giving them a toy to chew on will hopefully discourage them from chewing furniture and biting others, but it is important to remember that the puppy will still need to be educated as to what will be accepted and what won't.

When the puppy decides to bite or chew the wrong thing, it is important to stop it immediately by saying "no" in a firm voice and offer the puppy the opportunity to chew a toy.

At this stage it is important to identify whether the chewing and biting habits are just playful or something more serious. If the puppy shows signs of genuine aggression when playing then it's a good idea to avoid any form of rough play as this will only promote dominant behavior and result in more problems. Certain dog breeds can be more aggressive and you may need to consult a vet or an animal therapist if the chewing and biting cannot be solved.

Let's take a look at a few tips to stop chewing and biting.

Accept that the puppy will chew and purchase plenty of chew toys as alternatives to using the furniture.

Maintain consistency and offer praise when the puppy chews or bites the correct item.

Whenever the puppy bites or chews something other than their toy, respond with "no" and move the dog away from the offending object. Once this has been done, walk away from the dog and give it no attention.

When playing and giving attention to the puppy, try to avoid putting hands anywhere near the mouth as this will encourage biting.

If the puppy fails to respond to being told "no", consider using a water spray as an additional tool to shock the puppy, but avoid spraying the water anywhere near the eyes.

How to Train Your Puppy to Walk on a Leash

No matter what type of dog or puppy you own it is essential that you give it regular exercise. Different breeds have varying energy levels and some dogs will need to be walked more than once a day. An essential part of getting the dog to walk successfully will be training the puppy to accept the collar and leash (or lead) before you can attempt to walk anywhere.

The first stage of this training process is just about getting the puppy familiar with the collar. To begin with select a collar that is lightweight and not too bulky. Initially the puppy will show some form of resistance towards the collar, but leave it on for short periods and be sure not to remove the collar when the puppy is showing resistance. This is because it will begin to think that it has won the battle. If the puppy shows resistance towards the collar when you attempt to put it on, try putting it on when it's feeding or playing.

In time the puppy will accept the collar and you will be able to leave it on permanently and it's at this point you will then be able to bring in the leash. Initially, the best way to introduce the leash is to simply attach it to the collar and allow the puppy to walk around inside the house. Should the puppy show resistance, then adopt the same method as with the collar and attach the leash during feeding or playtime. When the puppy starts to accept the leash being attached, it's time to pick it up and follow them around.

Once the dog is happy with its new situation, then it's time to go outside and teach them how to behave on the leash. Now is the time that the basic commands such as sit, stop, stay and come will prove useful.

During the early stages of walking on a leash the puppy may pull on the leash in an attempt to guide you somewhere. Respond by jerking the leash and command the dog to "stop" and then "sit". If the puppy follows the command then offer praise and encouragement. Continue to apply this method whenever the dog pulls on the leash as it has to learn that when it does this, it will not be tolerated.

The same principle is applied if the puppy decides to stop walking and takes to sitting or lying down. Simply change the command to "come" and offer praise and encouragement when the puppy follows instruction.

Leash training requires tolerance and persistence and it won't happen overnight, but once you have mastered this technique it will make dog walking a far more pleasurable experience.

If you continue to experience problems when working your puppy on a leash, it may be worth discussing the situation with your vet and ask them to recommend a local dog obedience class as the bigger the puppy gets the more difficult it will be to train.

Puppy Games and Tricks

Playing games and teaching new tricks helps with a dog's development and promotes a better relationship between the owner and dog. Certain games can also be used as a useful training method.

The following list of games can be adapted to individual dogs, but the general idea is the same:

Fetch

Probably the most common game played between man and dog. Simply entertain the dog by throwing a ball and allow them to fetch. You may need to encourage the dog to bring the ball back at times, but after a while the dog will grasp the idea.

Follow the Leader

Use objects such as traffic cones, jumps, balls etc and encourage the dog to follow you through a particular path.

Find the Treat

Instruct the dog to sit and stay and then hide treats or their favorite toys around the house or garden. When you have finished hiding them, send the dog off to find them.

Hide and Seek

Whilst this may be a popular children's game it can be adapted for dogs. Get the dog to sit and wait until called. Then encourage him to find you or another family member.

Printed in Great Britain
by Amazon